Family Walks in Central Lakeland

by
Bob Swallow

Dalesman Books
1991

The Dalesman Publishing Company Ltd.,
Clapham, via Lancaster, LA2 8EB

First published 1991

© Bob Swallow 1991

ISBN: 1 85568 024 6

FOR PAULINE

Contents

Page

	Introduction	5
1.	Tewet Tarn, High Rigg and Castlerigg Stone Circle	7
2.	Dacre and Dalemain	11
3.	Howtown to Glenridding	15
4.	A Circuit of Gowbarrow Fell	21
5.	Lanty's Tarn and Greenside Mine	26
6.	A Circuit of Grasmere and Rydal Water	31
7.	Alcock Tarn	36
8.	Great and Little Langdale	39
9.	The Vale of St John's and High Rigg	45

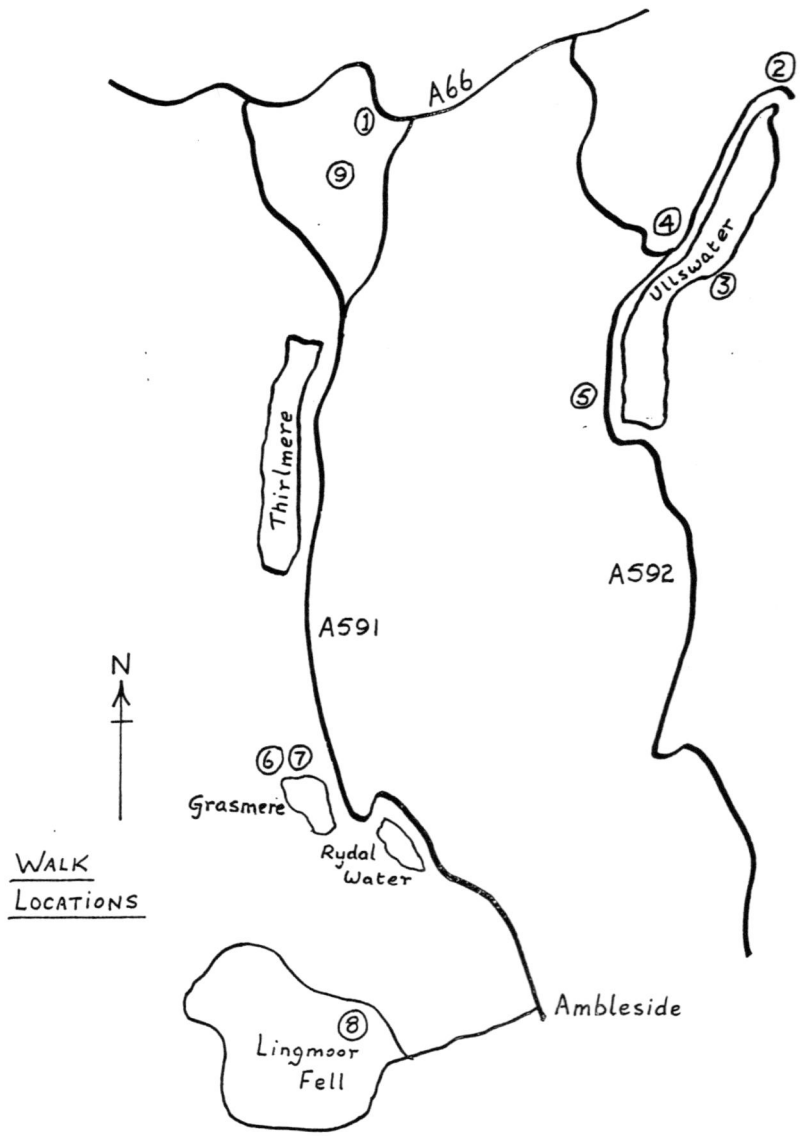

Introduction

THE Lake District needs little introduction, yet each year is invaded by an ever increasing band of tourists, some for the first time. There is little that has not been explored and researched in Lakeland and rather than simply detail the various walks, I have endeavoured to communicate to you, dear reader and walker, a little of the experiences which my friends and I have enjoyed over the years during the course of these easy expeditions.

We are a select band — Colin, myself, Stan and Bill — each separated from the next by some six years. As we have matured, our expeditions have become more discerning with frequent stops for sustenance, photography and even sound recording. Sustenance you will find classified into minor and major butty stops. At the former a flask top of tea and a biscuit is permitted whilst the latter allows for a three course meal. Generally the first half hour of a walk is spent putting the world to rights whilst gaining height. As the view expands (or sometimes contracts, depending on conditions) our thoughts move to a higher plane remote from politics, education, finance and the like. Memories flood back of previous occasions at the same or similar location in very different conditions. Crisp snow, an unforecast gale or a balmy summer morn when skylarks sing and all appears well with the world.

We are all devotees of that grand old gentleman of the fells, A. Wainwright, whose inspiration caused our family and doubtless many more to move north west. The walks are designed to appeal to all ages. They vary from 2½ to 8½ miles. Some barely leave the valley, others reach dramatic viewpoints. All tastes are catered for. Fellwalking boots are recommended, in fact a necessity. I write this with all the aplomb of one who has walked the dales and lakeland fells for forty years without serious mishap yet fell off his own rockery when endeavouring to prune a climbing rose and more significantly whilst wearing trainers. Ankle tendons and ligaments were damaged to such extent that it was not even possible to crawl ten yards to sanctuary of the house. So-called friends laughed like drains but at least the enforced rest permitted time to prepare this book and revisit past easy stamping grounds when recuperating.

I never went metric and it's getting a little late now. It follows that distance both horizontal and vertical are imperial measure. For the benefit of those brought up in a different school, one foot equals 0.3048 metres and one mile 1.6090 kilometres. Another benefit of non-metrication is that the mountains maintain their stature, it being far more impressive to announce the conquest of Scafell Pike at 3210 feet, rather than a measly 978 metres.

I have defined Central Lakeland for purposes of this book as being bounded by the A66 to the north, following the eastern shore of Ullswater thence over Kirkstone Pass to descend the old road to Ambleside. Westward the boundary skirts Loughrigg and Lingmoor Fells before striking north to meet the A66 once more east of Keswick. One or two of the walks stray over these arbitrary boundaries, but this is a book primarily intended for enjoyment and not a definitive work of art. Use it as an aid to a first tentative exploration or perhaps in later life after prolonged absence to search out more leisurely ways than those tackled during the first vigour of youth.

Thinking about youth, the fells are great places for young families. Our four children have all at some time been carried in a papoose, one of our sons later proudly topping all 214 fells detailed by Wainwright in his famous guides. This on his own legs and before his 14th birthday. Don't rush children, given their own time they are natural scramblers and also benefit from frequent stops near water where they may be relied upon to become both soaked and happy. Don't try rushing them round a fifteen mile circuit, it's self defeating. The enjoyment of the fells is rather in leisurely exploration, one eye always on the weather. The Lake District Weather Service is a good if not infallible guide. Ring it before setting forth, 096 62 5151.

My wife Pauline has never stood in my way, graciously granting successive Sunday passes perhaps strengthened by the knowledge that Sabbath spent on the fells makes me a marginally easier person with whom to live the following six days. Many of these walks we have trodden with our family, Howtown to Glenridding being a favourite. Now they are growing up the time may be near when once again the two of us get out into Lakeland on a more regular basis.

The walks are described clockwise starting with that to Tewet Tarn. The diagrams are intended to give an overall view of the walk relative to main centres and transport. Arm yourself with a copy of the relevant 1.25000 Ordnance Sheet, approximately 2½ inches to the mile and a work of art. No, I am not on commission and yes, they are good value.

Thinking back to my first tenuous steps in God's Country, I recall being initially intimidated by the mountains. Gradually, confidence gained, they became less so and my sorties more adventurous. Bear in mind we are talking about thirty years and more back when fellwalking was not the hi tech science which some have made it. A word of caution, always respect the fells and mountains, be prepared for the worst whilst hoping for better.

Oh, and like the man says, "Watch where you are putting your feet".

1. Tewet Tarn, High Rigg and Castlerigg Stone Circle

Start and Finish: Naddle Bridge adjacent A66, one and a half miles west of Threlkeld. A circular walk taking in a secluded tarn, a grand viewpoint and a stone circle of renown. Some rough walking but also meadowland.
Distance: 4½ miles.
Climbing: 900 feet.
Time: 3 hours.
Map: O.S. English Lakes 1.25000 North West.
Public Transport: C.M.S. Keswick/Penrith route 104 passes close to starting point on the newly aligned A66.

NADDLE BRIDGE spans Naddle Beck at what is now a quiet loop of road effectively relegated to layby status by progress. Not so long ago it formed a part of the A66 when that corkscrew of a route from Penrith to Keswick offered all the thrills of a roller coaster. Progress saw the easing of this corner into a more graceful curve, in its turn superseded by the modern highway bridging the River Greta by Britain's answer to the Europa Bridge, north east of Keswick. If road improvements do have benefits then here is one, a natural parking spot in an area of outstanding beauty surrounded by fine mountains and bang on the start of this walk.

Turn right or east as the fancy takes you, following this now deserted highway to its junction with its equally quiet mark one improvement where a sign points back to Castlerigg Stone Circle. Bearing right, continue for 200 yards past a presently untidy heap of spoil. A further sign indicates right, 'Diocesan Youth Centre, St John's in the Vale Church and Shundraw'. Wild rose; cow parsley; foxglove and wild geranium flower beneath hawthorn with its distinctive spring fragrance.

Beyond the double bend and through an avenue of trees take to the footpath indicated right for 'Tewit' Tarn. Tractor ruts swing gently uphill between enclosing walls passing a disused quarry, until, levelling out, Tewet Tarn is found nestling in a hollow. Named after the Peewit or Lapwing which can be seen in plenty hereabouts it is also the haunt of coot. Look closely for the fairly rare mountain pansy, a mini wild variety of the garden plant.

Westward, the stone circle to be visited later may be seen. Eastward, skirting the slopes of Clough Head, the northern terminus of the Helvellyn range, is the distinctive coach road from Threlkeld to Dockray. Coach road indeed, reaching 1420 feet with sections where coach passengers would, were they still inside, be lying flat on their backs, the title conjures up a ride of splendour not borne out by the

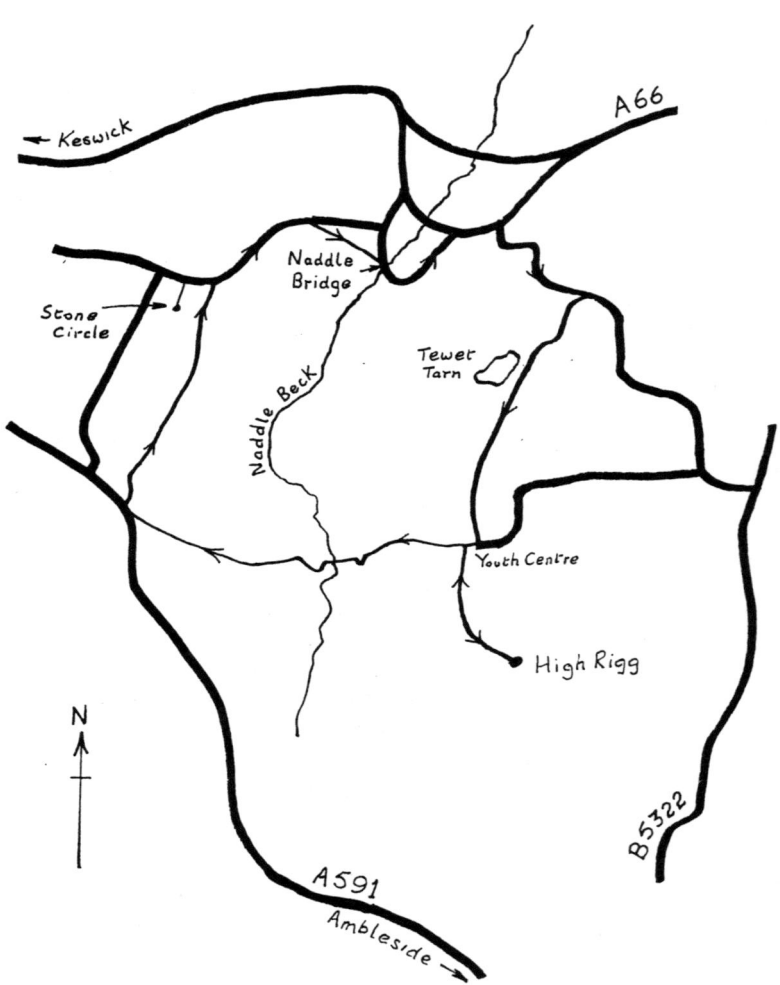

facts. All hands to the wheel would undoubtedly be the norm. Nonetheless it forms a link in a grand traverse of the Dodds starting at Dockray, travelling via the Brown Hills; Hart Side; Stybarrow Dodd; Watson's Dodd; Great Dodd and Clough Head before returning over its attractive (walking) course, all of fourteen miles.

Resolving to do all of that tomorrow, pass to the left of the tarn to cross a wall step stile near a barricaded gateway. The gently graded stone steps are a feature of many stiles on this walk. Keep to the topside of the intake wall ahead listening in season for skylark and cuckoo. Incline left to negotiate a fence by wooden step stile in a juicy depression, ascending later towards a solitary hawthorn. Tormentil stars peep through the grasses. The Carlisle Diocesan Youth Centre springs into view at a further wall, a distinct path leading to the complex of buildings which show signs in the stonework of recent extensions. To the left in trees is the turreted bell tower of St John's in the Vale Church, well worth a visit, though neglected by my muddy boots on the last occasion as a service was in progress.

To the right of the Diocesan Centre a steep path gains height quickly to pass through the intake wall at a kissing gate. From here the North Western Fells unfold in all their glory, Causey Pike and the ridge beyond being prominent. Further west is more remote country topped by Broom Fell with, hidden behind, the shy Wythop Woods from where Skiddaw thirty years back appeared to me as some undiscovered summit, Bassenthwaite Lake being lost to view at this point.

Continue upward on a velvet sward broken by yeti-like footprints. The church bell may be heard tolling eerily below. Blea Rigg's summit is easily gained and makes for a natural butty stop surrounded as it is by greater heights. Due east is Fisher Wife Rake beneath Wanthwaite Crags on Clough Head. Stan and I, together with Melvyn, a keen though inexperienced walker, made its ascent one grim and misty morning to Jim's Fold which Wainwright suggests, tongue in cheek, was the object of Fisher's wife's somewhat desperate ascents. Presumably she found a less arduous descent.

Retrace your steps towards the Youth Centre passing indigenous herdwick sheep suitably "rudded up" with Venetian Red be it the show season. Wheatear may be seen and heard in this stony landscape.

At the intake continue on a clear track, past a stand of mixed pines and sycamores dropping beyond to the rough road giving access to the church and centre from Dale Bottom. Note a hawthorn and beech intertwined above the entry to Sykes Farm. Leave the road at this point, taking direction from the footpath sign at a rocky outcrop. Keep to the height of land, oak trees to your left, before an abrupt descent to a kissing gate through which is easier ground.

A TV aerial grows forlornly in its own enclosure to your right.

Ahead stands a gate in splendid isolation. In this case, the hedge through which it originally permitted access has been removed to create a larger pasture. On the high fells there are several examples of similar gates in stark solitary splendour, marooned when the wire fences they breeched collapsed during the passage of time. The gates remain, supported by strong stretcher posts. On our nomadic travels it has become an invariable custom to pass through these gates no matter how difficult their opening may have become — and some mighty peculiar looks you get from other walkers who happen to be present. For our part, we offer greeting and smile sweetly giving to one and all the impression that it is the most natural thing in the world to struggle with a recalcitrant gate defending nothing in the midst of a wilderness. As they are mentioned in his guides, we have christened them, "Wainwright Gates".

Turn right, reassured by a footpath sign for Keswick. At a new fence veer left to cross Naddle Beck by narrow bridge. The route is now waymarked to the A591 emerging at a point where it is being realigned. After only fifty yards thankfully forsake it, crossing the cattle grid at the entry to Low Nest. Take to the field left over a step stile prior to passing a mobile hen house (right) and immobile domestic bath (left). Ascend the field to meet the tarmac drive leading to High Nest. Note the unusual metal-topped drainage channel bounding this drive. Thread the environs of High Nest leaving by gate beyond a barn with unusual cross set in a gable. Keep to the low side of the next field until, passing Scots Pines on your right, tackle the first of a series of stiles leading unfailingly to a minor road where turn left to find in 200 yards entry to Castlerigg Stone Circle, owned by The National Trust. A wealth of detail is available on site as to origins of the circle and how it was probably erected. There are similarities with the famous Easter Island statues in this latter context. This is an evocative spot in late afternoon during the shorter days as the sun dips low over Derwentwater, casting long broody shadows amidst the stones.

Retrace steps back down the lane continuing past the earlier point of emergence. Goose Well Farm on the left is a thriving riding school. From here Naddle Bridge is in view with hopefully your transport still in situ. The footpath shown on the 1.25000 map has been diverted to a point further north. Whilst seeking this on a recent visit, no less than 17 hang gliders were spotted on the slopes of Clough Head lined up as a squadron, taking off in relays, a colourful spectacle to round off this very varied walk as return is made to within ten yards of the bridge by a gate from the permissive footpath starting below Goose Well Farm.

2. Dacre and Dalemain

Start and Finish: Pooley Bridge astride B5320, five miles S.W. of Penrith. A lowland walk suitable for a day when the clouds are down on the high fells. The absence of steep climbing makes it ideal for grandparents, though perhaps I should qualify this remark bearing in mind there are these days many such only in mid thirties. Suitable for some grandparents, great grandparents and just possibly great great grandparents. Visiting the environs of a stately home; a renovated castle in a charming village and a church guarded by four bears.
Distance: 5 miles.
Climbing: estimated 400 feet.
Time: 3½ hours.
Map: O.S. English Lakes, 1.25000 North East.
Public Transport: C.M.S. Route 108 Penrith - Patterdale passes through Pooley Bridge. (No Sunday service).

POOLEY BRIDGE is host to a fund of fond memories, my first visit being over thirty years ago when staying with my future wife and in-laws at a battered caravan close to the lake's eastern shore. It was a full day's journey just to reach the village by rail and bus from Leeds. At that time Penrith sports took place on a field adjacent the Sun Inn. There was but one point of entry and exit from or to the Penrith road with the invariable result that local tractors and owners had a busy afternoon towing vehicles through the quagmire. The hastily prepared cycle and running track left something to be desired and would not have met World Championship standards. Nevertheless it somehow lost its appeal when transformed to a then more modern venue at Penrith.

Start from the parking area on the west bank of the river Eamont, following a good path north parallel with the river. Well tended gardens lead to the water's edge on the opposite bank. A mini island is passed, complete with its own mini bridge. Young children will love this. There are a plethora of seats adjacent the path. Wait a minute, surely you don't need one yet? Pink campion, foxglove and water forget-me-not are profuse. Go through a gate with notice confirming you are indeed on a footpath.

A weir with salmon leap maintains the lake level. Bear in mind water is extracted from Derwentwater, flowing by pipeline to Haweswater for onward transmission to Manchester's thirsty public, an underground journey over one hundred miles.

At the first step stile bear left on a new path avoiding excessively wet ground. There has been some engineering of this path to skirt a recent man-made tarn by provision of wooden walkways to avoid further wet stretches. The tarn is home to coots and boasts its own island. Trespassing is not encouraged, a newly planted belt of trees

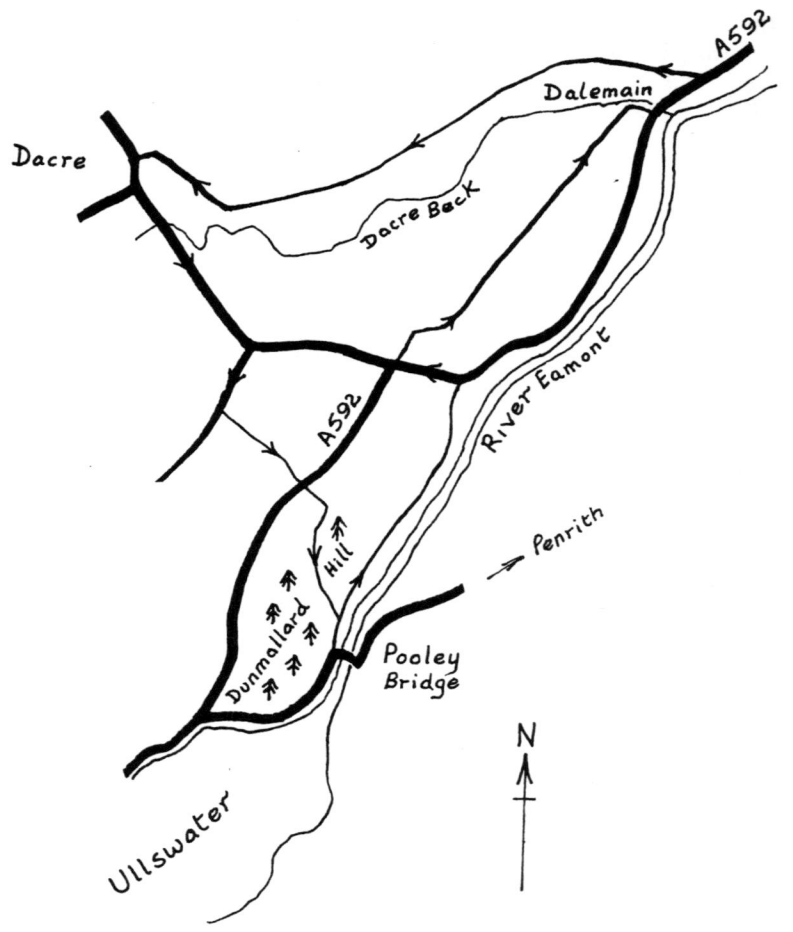

will eventually shield this stretch of water.

Join the A592 scurrying left for 150 yards to a junction where a minor road leaves for Dacre. An inviting sign announces, "Pub Grub". Well, not just yet . . . Climb a substantial red sandstone stile right, to enter pasture. Within yards a further wooden stile requires tackling with care, both stile and fence being unsafe. Thankfully the next fence and even more rickety stile have collapsed, though sufficient remains to make out a directional arrow.

Topping a rise, look back to Pooley Bridge's own sentinel, Dunmallard, a low but distinctive hill clothed in mixed woodland. Beyond lies Barton Fell straddled by the Roman Road, "High Street" bound for Ambleside via its highway in the clouds, the lower reach of Ullswater contrasting with easy pastures running to its fringe. Arable land to your left is followed by a shelter belt of trees from which the stately home Dalemain may be seen across Dacre Bridge. Crossing Dalemain Park, no clear route is evident, head right to a step stile, rejoining the A592 to permit a crossing of Dacre Beck by the ballustraded road bridge. Follow the road to the vehicular access for this historic property open to the public in season. Perhaps now is not the time whilst wearing muddy boots but bear it in mind for the future.

Beyond the car park a children's play area will be seen on the right before entering the courtyard beneath an arch. Stonecrop and lichen make a colourful addition to the stonework. Refreshments are available, including bar lunches.

Leave by wide track accompanying the high garden wall. No chance of a sly peep in from here. The easy path continues through woodland, Dacre Beck in close proximity. At Kennel Cottage two mares and a pony trotted over to make friends.

Arable land takes over, flanked on your right by an avenue of trees. Wild rose and meadow vetchling (a yellow variety of tufted vetch) give a summer splash of colour. At a gate where the route veers a few points west, Dacre Castle will be seen in a commanding position. It was in fact one of many Pele Towers protecting the Eden Valley from cross border rids. For many years it lay in somewhat dilapidated condition before being purchased and renovated by the Kinsman family. A book with the intriguing title "Pawn takes Castle" tells of its conversion to an albeit unusual private dwelling.

There is further defence for the castle in the form of a particularly glutinous stretch of track near a heap of silage at the foot of a short rise where inevitably tractors have churned the ground. Never mind, it's a good clean country smell or so I've been informed many times. Rubbish! Try slipping in the stuff. It's a good test of true love as to whether your partner will assist you back to terra firma — let alone wash your gear!

Pass farm outbuildings to your left and the castle likewise to enter Dacre village. This is a little gem. There is a seat opposite junction of track and tarmac road beneath a tree fronting Rose Cottage. Strains of Schubert's Unfinished Symphony drifted by as I enjoyed a minor butty stop comprising apple and cuppa. Hungry walkers should be sure of a warm welcome, a hot potato trailer being parked outside the cottage. The village boasts a telephone box; post box; post office and a public house — the one that advertised, "Pub Grub" back on the A592. So you will be well provided for. Having satisfied secular needs, visit Dacre Parish Church, up the hill and right on to a short lane where wild raspberries grow. Like the castle it is a sandstone building and deceptively large inside. Everyone knows the story of the three bears. Well, Dacre Church goes one better with a story (and bears to back it) about four of them. It's all in a short history of the building which can be purchased by honest donation within for 50p. Go on, it won't break you.

Descend the hill to Low Bridge over which is quaintly named Lord's Waste Access Area administered by the Lake District National Park. Now comes the tough part of this relatively level walk, up a hill advertised as 1 in 8, or for the younger generation 12½%, this seeming somehow less severe. Five minutes later, at the brow, the real Lakeland represents itself. Arthur's Pike; Bonscale Pike; Pikewassa (lovely name) building up impressively above Ullswater.

Take a right turn, still on tarmac, for Soulby and, within 300 yards a bridleway left, bound once more for the A592. Several notices reassure this is, "Path to Dacre" and by implication from Pooley Bridge. Cross the highway to join a bridleway. At the top of the rise look carefully for a step stile topped by white post. Two more should be seen over rising ground, the second giving access to Dunmallard and its wood. Most will turn left on the direct route. Great great grandparents blessed with a surfeit of energy may take the circular route back to point of departure and attractions of Pooley Bridge.

3. Howtown to Glenridding

Start and Finish: Glenridding. A walk which uniquely commences on the deck of a "steamer", travelling by water to Howtown on the eastern shore of Ullswater. Thence through contrasting scenery around the foot of Hallin Fell. Return is by a small amount of road walking to Glenridding.
Distance: 7 miles.
Climbing: Estimated 400 feet.
Time: 4½ hours.
Map: O.S. English Lakes 1.25000 North East.
Public Transport: C.M.S. service Penrith/Patterdale, route 108. (No Sunday service). Mountain Goat bus from Ambleside (Twice daily in season).

THIS is a walk which I have completed in part many many times as section of a round trip based on Patterdale, climbing Place Fell, returning via Sandwick. It might with two cars be accomplished from Howtown to Glenridding omitting the cruise. Undoubtedly, however, the route par excellence is by taking the "steamer" — it used to be just that — from Glenridding to Howtown thus having the most dramatic scenery to the fore on the return.

Bill and I did just this one glorious July day, the sort you dream of. For starters the crew of "Lady of the Lake" turned out to be as nice a bunch as you would hope to meet anywhere, the two lady members supplying thirst-quenching drinks the moment we left shore. Captain Nick Smith then invited us into the wheelhouse where we learned he had only been with the company four months, previously operating an Isle of Wight ferry in one of the world's busiest shipping lanes. His wife is "in computers" in Penrith and an ambition has been fulfilled to get away from the rat race. As we swung towards Howtown a flight of mallard accompanied our course, settling on the water with respective broods as berthing took place. Nick promptly revealed the reason, producing a bag of left-over bread provided by friends in Patterdale. A 10.35 breakfast is the norm for these birds. Nick went on to tell us of one brood of merganser that numbered thirteen and also how the peregrines appear as if by appointment Saturdays only.

Leaving the pier, cross the bridge over Fusedale Beck where it enters Ullswater, then follow the shore, here lined with silver birch. Harebell and yarrow grow at your feet. The cairn on Arthur's Pike is prominent on the mass of Barton Fell, itself sweeping down to the lake's eastern shore. Pikewassa seen "end on" bisects Fusedale from Bannerdale. This is red deer country. The Martindale zig-zags may be seen climbing to the new church serving the needs of one of the smaller parishes in the country, less than one hundred souls. One icy morning I contrived to slide a car sideways down the bends, ending up at right angles across the cattle grid at the bottom. Shanks pony

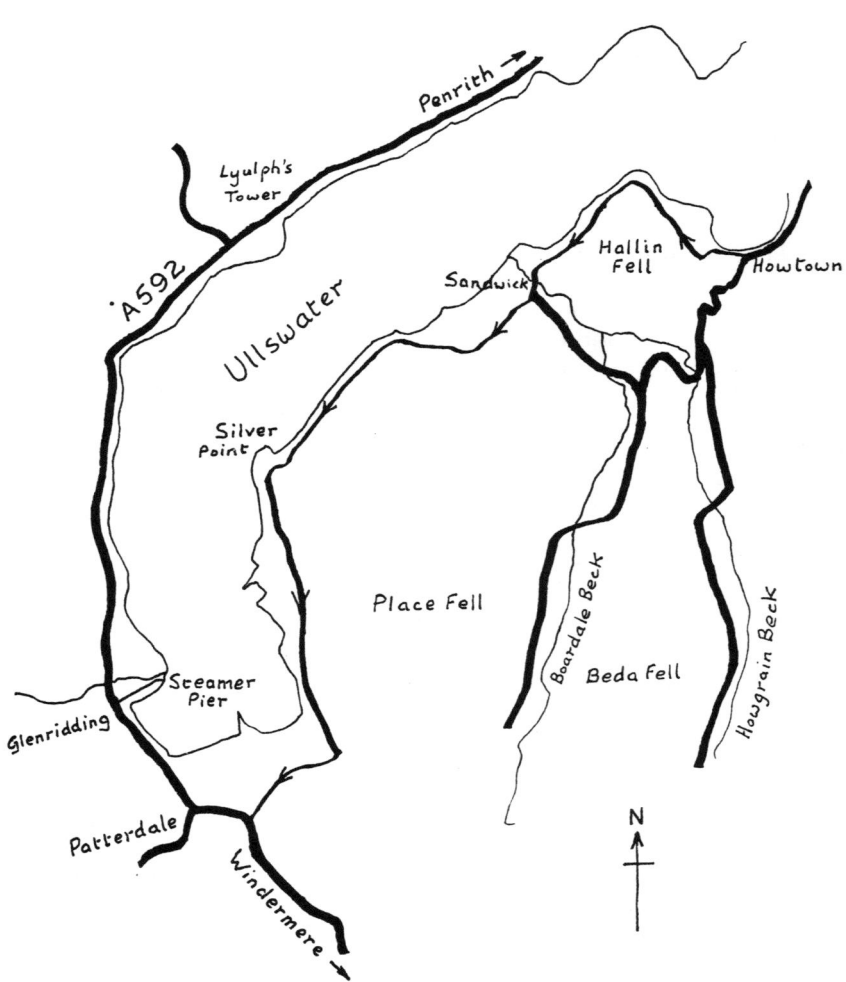

became order of that particular day.

There are kissing gates before a signposted left turn leads up steep steps lined by foxgloves and lichen covered walls to a terrace above the intake wall. Left leads via "the Rake" to the summit of the road and Hallin Fell. Our course goes right, now with sweeping views down the pastoral reach of Ullswater, Pooley Bridge backed by Dunmallet, shown on recent maps as Dunmallard Hill. Pass a strategic seat encompassing the view before swinging west to Kailpot Crag. Here set into the sheer rock face and only visible from the water, a plaque commemorates Lord Birkett who in 1962 successfully fought in the Upper House to maintain the lake as just that and not allow it to be turned into a reservoir as promoted by Manchester Corporation Waterworks Department. It has to be admitted that water is now extracted for that city but this is effected unobtrusively passing by pipeline from below the surface level. Birkett Fell near Hart Side also remembers this Peer's efforts. He died shortly after the bill was defeated in 1962.

Hallinhag Wood clothes the next half mile with sessile oak; beech and ash in abundance, great terrain for tree creepers and woodpeckers. Sunlight dances on moss and fern through thick foliage. The track is consolidated by boulders and horizontal lengths of felled timber creating a now mature and durable footpath.

A sandy beach at the far end of the wood provides an excellent minor butty stop sheltered by a shallow bay. We sat on the warm sand, Bill recalling a not dissimilar situation in the Yorkshire Dales when a brazen pheasant had appeared as from nowhere to snatch a tomato sandwich from his hand before making back to cover, later to return and polish off a scotch egg. The general peace is shattered by the occasional outboard motor, a comparative rarity on Ullswater which caters almost exclusively for sailing craft plus an increasing number of colourful sailboards.

An open stretch follows by a sign Howtown/Sandwick. A newly cut field supported an amazing floral border including meadow wood cranesbill; clover; betony and tansy. The lake shore is here forsaken to head inland, bearing right to the bridge over sun-flecked Boardale Beck, spanning a geological fault of Skiddaw slate and Borrowdale volcanic rock.

The sound of shearing wafted from a farm where we were permitted to watch professionals at work. Two young men, one spending six months a year back home in the Falklands, the other a Scottish champion, teaming up to work their way northwards during the season with a conglomeration of Emett-like equipment including a conveyor system into which sheep were fed by helper, queuing up at shoulder height behind two spring loaded vertical opening gates operated by the shearers. Clippers were connected by flexible cable not unlike a petrol pump. I did a time and motion job prior to their breaking for lunch. Fifty seconds per sheep plus ten further to despatch and grab the next. Pay is per head or perhaps tail, this latter requiring a delicate touch to strip without harm. It seemed somehow indecent haste after a twelve month of growing. At the time of writing, wool prices are at rock bottom, doubtless aided by a succession of mild winters. Imagine visiting the hairdresser to be advised, "I shan't be a minute" and meaning it. On this basis a mere head should be about a ten second job and cost a copper or two.

Walk a few yards up the tarmac lane to where a sign for Patterdale gives direction right on an easy track standing back from the lake and some hundred feet above it. Place Fell is now building up on the left, a path leading off to tackle this prior to our descent and crossing of Scalehow Beck which, if followed upstream, would lead almost to the summit at 2154 feet.

Our course heads north west above Scalehow Wood on steeper volcanic slopes before returning to a south westerly bearing. Across the lake lies Gowbarrow Fell with in the foreground Lyulph's Tower, a castellated hunting lodge. An easily graded path climbs behind the lodge across the face of the fell before circling to its summit. The Helvellyn range is building up aggressively, often cloud topped. Again the climate may vary considerably down the length of the lake. Indeed, whilst Bill and I had set off in glorious sunshine at Howtown, the sky ahead was now looking decidedly ominous. South of Gowbarrow Fell and separated by the road to Troutbeck are the Brown Hills swinging easily from Matterdale End to Glencoynedale backed by Sheffield Pike. Stan and I once had to retreat from this area during an absolute whiteout. Catstycam marks the limit of Swirral Edge descending from Helvellyn.

Amazing the apparel worn on the fells these days. Long black skirts and floral pants headed in the opposite direction. For sheer colour though come this way in the autumn, the last two weeks in October to see it at its very best. The trees that is, not the pants.

The path now continues an undulating course across steeply sloping ground, though the scree is stabilised by birch; rowan and juniper, the latter sometimes mistaken for yew. This stretch is known as Birk Fell Earth suggesting a haven for foxes.

A promontory, Silver Point, has an almost Caribbean air, the sheltered shingle anchorage to a handful of small craft on a calm day. It might almost be a Treasure Island beach and well worth scrambling down from the main path for ten minutes siesta.

An alternative route breaks away left at a large cairn to climb behind the point by higher course. Stay on the lower path for superior views. The character of this walk changes yet again as the track moves to easier ground though back from the shoreline. Small islets dot the lake, home to cormorants. Gulls abound, heron and coot may also be sighted.

A bevy of horseriders made their way past that July day, outward bound from Side Farm our next port of call where there is a small shop supplying drinks and ices. Turn right to take an unmetalled road crossing Goldrill Beck to join the A592. Right again and almost opposite is Patterdale Church which will repay a visit. A glorious tapestry hangs inside, Christ depicted as a shepherd surrounded by well known local fells. A couple of herdwicks and lambs are at his feet. The chalice contains silver from the former Greenside Mine.

A short stretch of road walking is inevitable though a path has been cut through woodland where the lake encroaches. As the landing stage comes into view take a short cut near a lake shore snack bar to return to point of departure having completed one of Lakeland's classic walks.

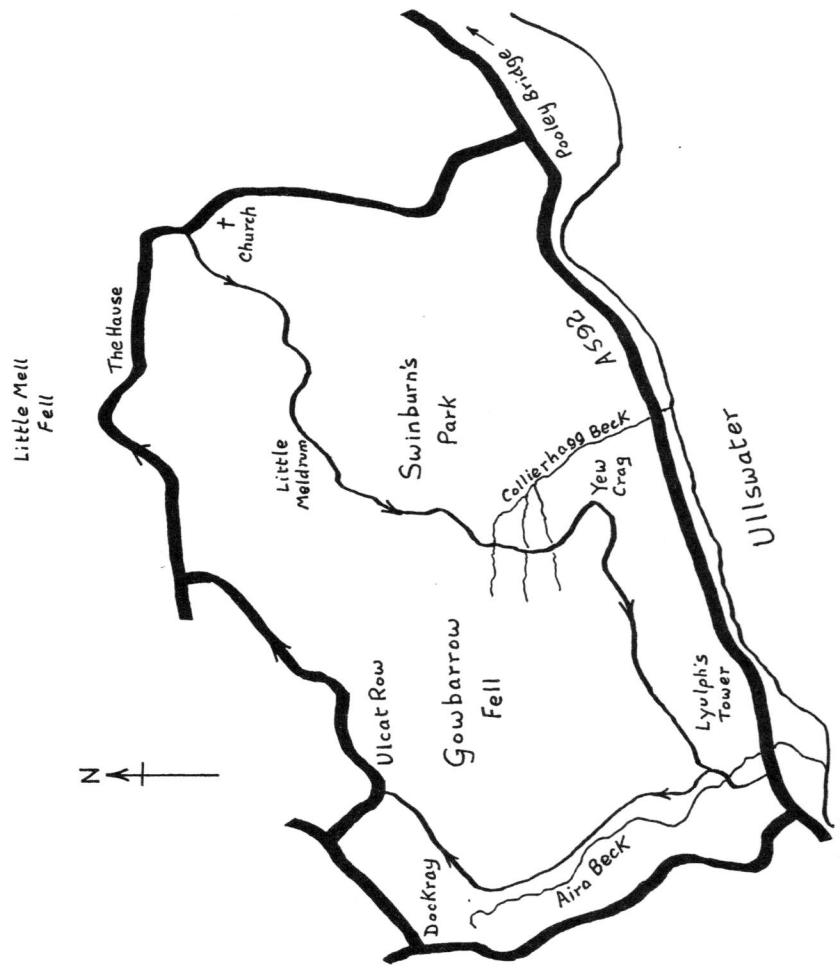

4. A Circuit of Gowbarrow Fell

Start and Finish: National Trust car park 300 yards north east of the Dockray junction on A592 beside the northern shore of Ullswater. Spectacular early views on the climb beside Aira Beck and waterfalls followed by open country and a spell on quiet single track lanes. Return is by increasingly airy traverse through Swinburn's Park and around the eastern and southern flanks of Gowbarrow Park.
Distance: 8 miles.
Climbing: 1300 feet.
Time: 5½ hours.
Map: O.S. English Lakes 1,25000 North East.
Public Transport: C.M.S. route 108 Penrith/Patterdale (No Sunday service).

AIRA FORCE forms a dramatic introduction to this walk. It is within Gowbarrow Park which together with Glencoyne Wood is owned by the National Trust and extends to almost 3650 acres including 2½ miles on the shore of Ullswater.

Walk to the head of the car park passing through a gate with novel closing mechanism. The first of many such. A good path has been provided to the next gate adjacent to which a National Trust notice refers to the original Victorian planting scheme in the locality. Over an extended period the Trust are endeavouring to replant on a selective basis with more broadleaved trees. The Victorians had planted several decorative varieties such as Himalayan Fir; Deodar Fir and Chilean Pine (monkey puzzle). There are also many rhododendrons.

Where the path forks, go right, descending through parkland provided with seats to a substantial wooden footbridge over Aira Beck, here set in a deep ravine. Climb the far bank by a flight of awkwardly spaced steps. When the path splits, take the lower alternative noting an amazing conifer, one limb growing out horizontally for some fifteen feet before abruptly turning heavenward. What caused such contortions? In fact there are several grotesque trees lining the path which has an almost sheer drop on the left to the beck below. Young children should be kept on a tight rein here.Descend to a packhorse type bridge to the right of which a plaque commemorates Cecil Spring Rice CCMG GCVO H.M. Ambassador to the U.S.A. during World War I. Stop on the bridge for a spectacular view of Aira Force tumbling 65 feet from beneath a higher bridge. Stan, who accompanied me whilst preparing notes on this walk pointed out the contrast in construction, the lower being built with all stones unusually in vertical format whilst the higher is of more traditional style incorporating horizontal stonework above the arch. The Force is a difficult subject to photograph being enclosed by trees.

Now back on the west bank, climb a further flight of steps pausing to take in even better views of this well known waterfall. At the top of the steps join a further path bearing right to look down upon the lower bridge.

Paradoxically, descend slightly to the higher bridge. Confusing, isn't it? Don't worry it will all fall into place when you see it. Talking of falling, try hard not to topple over the parapet as you compare contrasting views left and right, the latter being the dramatic plunge to lower bridge. The high bridge too boasts a plaque, not to be outdone. Built by friends in memory of Edward Spring Rice C.B. 1856–1902.

Once more on the east bank follow the left hand track above turbulent waters, ignoring paths to higher levels. Pass through a gate again with chain and weight closer. A viewpoint follows, where on a peninsula of land, the beck changing direction below has scoured a channel deep into living rock. A further bridge will be seen but our course now remains on the eastern side after zig-zagging upward to avoid difficult ground near this point.

The area is rich in mosses, ferns and lichens. Dippers frequent the beck, whilst flycatchers and tree creepers may also be sighted. The red squirrel is still found in the predominantly oak woods.

Approach the High Force still in woodland, soon to reach a gate bearing the notice, "Footpath to Dockray and Ulcat Row – please keep to path – all dogs on lead. Farmland".

Woodland thins and beyond another wall gives way to open heath, the bracken slope leading to the summit of Gowbarrow Fell. This is a marked change in terrain to open countryside. The valley seen left leads to the isolated farmstead of Dowthwaite Head, the slopes of Great Dodd beyond. A slight descent brings another lone dwelling into view set in an oasis of lush green grass, a converted former mill in idyllic setting where Riddings Beck meets Aira Beck.

At a three armed signpost opt for the faint track for Ulcat Row following the topside of a wall. At a further gate a notice entreats you to , "Please be sure to shut the gate". Reminds me of a similar one I read down Garsdale many years back.

"Be ye soon or be ye late
Be yer sure to shut the gate".

The track swings to a near easterly bearing. Ahead should be seen Little Mell Fell and left, coming into view from behind conifers, Great Mell Fell. Up on the fellside a flock of this year's lambs looking in fine fettle were being shepherded by a young farmer and trainee dog. Piercing whistles and tongue to match rent the air. Prior to meeting tarmac at Ulcat Row, pass to the rear of a fine old farmhouse enjoying views towards Blencathra, a pyracantha growing lustily in its sheltered corner despite being on the 1000 foot contour. A grotesque half-collapsed larch forms an arch over the track.

Through a gate join the minor road, going straight ahead whilst on the right a former chapel is being tastefully converted to living accommodation. There are more properties, one being extended, and some rum names, "Laal Steans" for example. Follow the delightful lane which is quiet and virtually traffic free for a good mile to a "T" junction. Here turn right towards Watermillock. This section over half a mile is an ascending drag which there is no avoiding. Best foot forward and get it over. Better, much better lies ahead. The Hause is a col at the summit of the road. A footpath leads left as though to tackle Little Mell Fell. Should you cross the roadside stile to another at the base of the fell, a sign there indicates a path to Lowthwaite and another which reads, "No access to fell above here". Despite this, on an earlier visit we met a church party bound for the summit apparently to hold a brief service.

Back on the road a swinging descent leads past woods left where a notice on a Scots Pine "Beware Adders" leads one to think there is little welcome on the hillsides hereabouts. Ullswater can be glimpsed, and beyond, Barton Fell, the precursor to High Street, the greatest altitude on the Far Eastern Fells at 2718 feet.

Ignore the road left bound for Bennet Head and Dacre, a static caravan site lies on the same side before our route turns due south to approach a former school, again on the left. Just prior to this but on the opposite side a path starts at a gate, climbing beneath Priest's Crag, sheltered in trees below being Watermillock Church and rectory. This is our course, the view across Ullswater gradually widening to encompass the fine ridge from Askham to Ambleside.

Climb to a col near Gate Crags below which is Hagg Wood. A little further, gorse was still in flower on December 2nd. The path narrows, breeching a wall via kissing gate. Here enter the environs of the Economic Forestry Group, "Don't start fire, Dial 999". From where for heavens sake? In the lea of Little Meldrum beneath a hawthorn bough is an ideal butty stop. Visit it soon for the view, otherwise rapidly encroaching young fir will have blotted it out. Hallin Fell presently leads the eye to Place Fell followed by Beda Fell; The Nab and Rest Dodd. Hopefully replete, continue into Swinburn's Park where the going becomes muddy, indeed treacherous for a short stretch.

The track now heads south west, from this fresh angle Howtown Bay can be seen, calling point for Ullswater "steamers". For the better part of two miles and almost to the end of this walk the track will hug the contour around 1200 feet. Young conifers encroach much too close. Surely it would have been possible to have left a belt of open ground adjacent to the track.

The summit of Gowbarrow Fell with a distinctive cairn is now ahead on the skyline. Before a further wall is an EFG sign "Swinburn's Park" on which someone has scrawled "Kill Sitka Spruce". Not me, I hasten to add, though I share their sentiments. Cross a ladder stile from where Gowbarrow summit may be gained by either following the wall right or taking a beeline ahead up the slope. Although the track we are on is the only official right of way on what is now National Trust land, access is freely permitted to the public subject only to conservation and farming needs.

Opt left at the ruins of an old shooting box, climbing slightly to cross the first of three feeders collectively forming Collierhagg Beck. Immediately a bridge spans a landslip. Heading now almost due south decision time looms once more at a bifurcation. Go left for a further highlight of the walk. Ullswater is now in close proximity with the A592 highway seemingly beneath your feet round the headland of Yew Crag. Should you have any butties left this is the spot to eat them, a slab seat being conveniently to hand. Over a step stile the view is even better, looking into the head of the lake. On that December day a Sea King helicopter, R.A.F. Rescue hovered into view below us as sunshafts broke from a low orb behind the angle of Place Fell. The Helvellyns were still obliterated by mist. The chopper swung into Grisedale apparently on a mercy mission. Later we saw it hovering above Heron Pike where a tricky descent starts from Sheffield Pike to Glenridding.

The track takes an easy gradient from Yew Crag, so there should be no need for rescue at this point. Lyulph's Tower is seen from above, the home of the Howard Family and built during the 1780's as a hunting lodge which presumably accounts for the castellated facade as seen from the lake. It must be emphasised that the tower is private property not owned by the National Trust.

Reaching level ground look left, a step stile allowing return to the outward route above the wooden footbridge. Notice the gnarled remains of an ancient tree, its blanched limbs pock-marked with woodpecker holes. Return to the car park via the footbridge where youngsters will enjoy crawling through the fallen and hollowed trunk of another tree. Go on, be a devil, crawl through yourself — just to prove you can still do it.

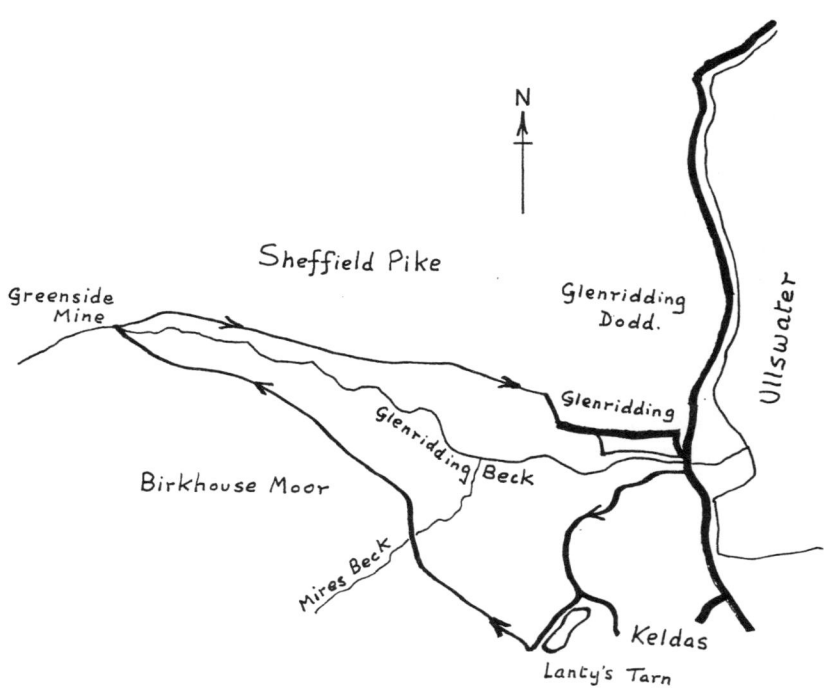

5. Lanty's Tarn and Greenside Mine

Start and Finish: Glenridding car park. Climbing initially to a grand viewpoint overlooking Ullswater, descending to an idyllic tarn and traversing a fellside path to the site of the former Greenside lead mine. Return is by easy metalled lane.
Distance: 4 miles.
Climbing: Estimated 900 feet.
Time: 3½ hours.
Map: O.S. English Lakes 1.25000 North East.
Public Transport: C.M.S. Route 108 Penrith–Patterdale. No Sunday service. Mountain Goat from Ambleside, twice daily in season.

GLENRIDDING sits astride the A592 linking Windermere via Kirkstone Pass with Penrith. It boasts an enormous pay car park, although the ticket issuing machines are not always reliable. If in difficulty, call at the imposing information centre, where, on a last visit the lady in charge kindly provided sheet of paper and pen to leave a note pleading mitigation. It worked. Makes it seem just like home doesn't it?

Return to the main road, bearing right to cross Glenridding Bridge. There is a plethora of shops supplying food and drink or even boots and cags should you require instant kit. Follow the beck upstream passing the public hall on your right. Several renovated properties flank the lane many with delightful gardens sporting clematis, honeysuckle and wild rose.

Beyond "Glenkeld" the route bifurcates, a sign inviting walkers to take either course. That to the left is an invitation to younger members of the family, being a summer crawl through overhanging bushes. Parents and grandparents will opt for that to the right. No matter, their courses rejoin within 100 yards! The path climbs steeply beneath beeches, having been improved in recent years by a series of zig-zags easing the gradient, at small expense by increased distance.

At a left turn recover your breath by stopping to admire tantalising glimpses of Ullswater. Pass through a kissing gate near an erosion control notice. Moving into more open country the path leads through bracken and foxgloves, Greenside Mine complex coming into view round the angle of Birkhouse Moor. Sheffield Pike forms the backdrop, its screes descending in chaos to the old workings. Further east its lower satellite Glenridding Dodd descends steeply to the lake.

A hand rail accompanies the path in its upper reaches. Ignore an inviting gate through a wall, continuing upward until a level sward is underfoot. Place Fell dominates the far lake shore with Silver Point on a promontory, beyond which the water's course swings from north to north east. The lakeside path may be clearly seen and is described in another chapter. Gowbarrow Fell sweeps to the western shore of this middle reach.

A short descent brings Lanty's Tarn into view through its shelter of mixed pine and deciduous trees. At small extra effort, you should tackle Keldas, only a few hundred yards uphill through the wall gap to your left. Be certain to have your camera handy for dramatic views of the lake from this pine dotted summit. *Raven* and *Lady of the Lake* plough their course in season back and forth between Glenridding and Pooley Bridge, calling at Howtown. Wainwright eulogises over this spot, with good cause.

Return by same route to the tarn, passing through a kissing gate to gain its western shore. Although man-made as a mini reservoir, it is a gem. At the far end I always stop for a cuppa to drink in the view up Grisedale toward the Helvellyn range. Midweek on the right day, you can listen to the silence. During summer, bees and crickets break it, a soughing wind may ripple water sheltered by birch. This is a good place to put the world to rights.

Leave arcadia by narrow track climbing half right from the dam wall, soon crossing a depression with circular cattle feed contraption in view. Head for a gate on the skyline. Arriving, use the adjacent step stile to cross the wall. Looking back, Keldas is in clear view. Perhaps you will hear the Patterdale foxhounds baying from their kennels. Now the view up the Glenridding valley beckons. Strange that it is not known as Glenriddingdale, sandwiched as it is between Grisedale and Glencoynedale, though Glenridding itself was but a cluster of properties prior to mining swelling the need for accommodation.

Cross an area of outcropping rock, moving right to find a faint trod descending steeply to easier though muddy ground. This is soon negotiated beyond which the route continues to meet and accompany a wall to Miresbeck. Here cross a now clear path coming up from Rattlebeck Bridge, it continuing over the summit of Birkhouse Moor to Helvellyn either by Striding or Swirral Edge.

Back during 1975, Stan and I tackled Helvellyn via the north east ridge of Birkhouse Moor as described by Wainwright from a point slightly north of the beck and adjacent to the course of an overflow from a former water race which in turn fed a pipeline driving equipment down at Rattlebeck. It was a misty day and a route took careful picking through bracken and outcrop. Real ankle ricking stuff, not made easier in the thin light of dawn. Reaching the summit, we seemed doomed to disappointment view-wise until suddenly, as through parted curtains, Catstycam was revealed. As quickly it disappeared. Yet within five minutes the whole area was bathed in sunlight, from Striding Edge round to Swirral Edge and Catstycam, Red Tarn set as a pink jewel in the morning glow. All the more memorable as we had the place to ourselves.

Continue on a clear path, the wall still on your right. A bifurcation is reached. All decisions isn't it? The higher choice leads to the course of the former water race previously mentioned. This is the best bet, following the lie of land unerringly and being at great elevation enjoying a wider view. The race was cut as recently as 1928. From here the scale of mining activity becomes apparent.

Mining began as early as 1650, though the complex of buildings remaining date back to only mid 19th century when Greenside was the largest lead mine in England. Silver was a derivative, some finding its way into church use at Patterdale. The Lucy Tongue level on the 1100 foot contour actually passed in an arc beneath Sheffield Pike to emerge in Glencoyndale. Cottages were provided for the workers in this latter valley, appropriately named Seldom Seen. There are also some on the opposite lower flank of our valley, many now being holiday homes.

During the First World War, Italian P.O.Ws. worked the mine from a special camp. During the second, local men provided five sevenths of all lead mined in the country. As early as 1890 electric locomotives were in use within the mine complex.

A plantation helps stabilize land on this side of the valley, attempts opposite have been made to halt the steady progress of scree, these meeting with only limited success where a thin covering of grass is taking tenuous hold. Glenridding Screes are themselves an impressive sight, the parent fell Sheffield Pike being well worth a visit for the views of Ullswater. Glenridding Dodd may also be visited on descent but do not as I have take a bee line through the woods to the lake shore. It is excessively rough and not worth fracturing an ankle trying to save half an hour.

The lower path rejoins before swinging south West, opening up a view to Catstycam and Helvellyn Lower Man. Glenridding Beck boils in its ravine spanned by footbridge. Cross this noting the array of weirs and sluices. The miners made excellent use of their readily available source of power, seven tons of water being required for every ton of ore mined. One and threequarter miles upstream a dam was formed at Keppel Cove. It burst during October 1927 swamping Glenridding village and almost finishing the mining company which had to pay compensation.

Some years back, again with surveyor friend Stan, I inspected the remains of this dam after descending the north west ridge of Catstycam.

You need an excuse for rest after this just to make sure your knee joints still operate. Looking at the remains of the dam wall, Stan opined it was little wonder it had failed the test of time due to its inferior construction.

Entering the complex, a general tidying up has taken place since final closure in 1961. Temporary buildings were removed the following year but many others have found fresh use. One, an outward bound centre, noticably sporting a "Dirty boots entrance". There is a Youth Hostel, well sited for the Helvellyn range, and, no less required, Mountain Rescue post. Youngsters will take short cuts omitting gradient easing zig-zags through the former works. Parents and grandparents will doubtless chastise them whilst remembering days when they did likewise.

Return to Glenridding is by part metalled lane. A building on the left set back into the hillside below the workings suggests a former explosives store. Soon the cottages mentioned earlier will be passed, now spruced up, afternoon teas being taken in front gardens on a good day. A splendidly sited Silver Jubilee seat offers respite for tired limbs, and, little further the Travellers Rest may tempt other walkers. Perhaps after all 3½ hours is not too long for this very varied walk.

Return to the car park after passing further properties on the right, noting the gable ends of some tile hung against the prevailing westerlies. A short cut leads through the grounds of the health centre. Let's hope you do not have cause to visit this too.

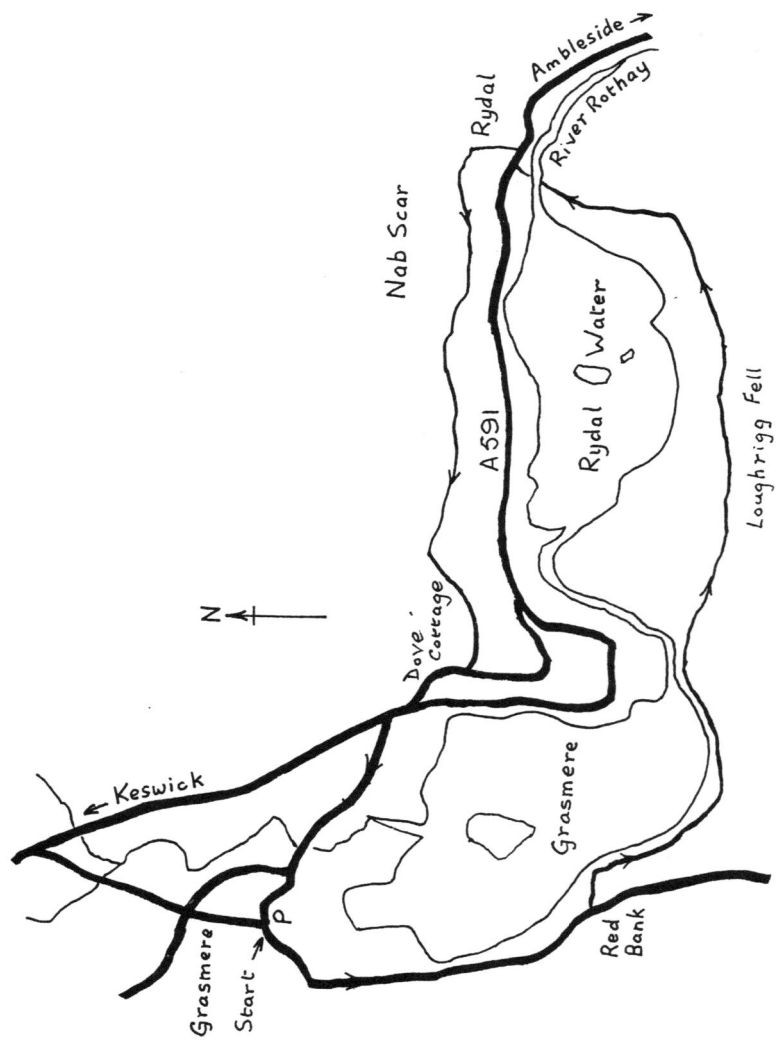

6. A Circuit of Grasmere and Rydal Water

Start and Finish: Grasmere, Red Bank Road car park. Circumventing these two idyllic sheets of water by woodland path, shingle shore and quiet lane. Visiting also a huge man-made cave on Loughrigg Fell.
Distance: 5½ miles.
Climbing: 400 feet.
Time: 4 hours.
Map: O.S. English Lakes 1.25000 South East.
Public Transport: C.M.S. Routes 555; 556; 557. Lancaster/Keswick.

RED BANK ROAD has a long stay car park sited at the western edge of Grasmere village. A slate sign and arrow indicates "To Boats" at the entrance. Take direction from this, following the metalled lane around the western shore of Grasmere. The boat launch pier is passed, only rowing and sailing varieties being permitted. There is an island almost in the centre about which Bill recalls a tale concerning the then Prince of Wales. He apparently rowed out to the island where he was seen by an elderly lady to be riding rodeo style a good sized tup. She remonstrated with him, being in turn taken to task by a member of his retinue. Did she not know he was the Prince of Wales? "No matter if he is," she is alleged to have replied, "he is an ill mannered brat." So are the mighty fallen.

As the road ascends Red Bank, look north to Dunmail Raise flanked on the left by Steel Fell and right Seat Sandal, both sporting excellent ridges from Grasmere. The latter was incidentally our younger son's last peak in the Wainwright guide series, number 214, he being just 14 at the time. That same day Bill had set forth with Stan and I for the first time. (It was nearly his last, after a heavy fried breakfast the direct ascent of Red Screes from Kirkstone being very much a red mist job). Red Bank is so called for the colours which adorn it in autumn, possibly the finest time of year to tackle this walk. Some years back you may recall a TV series based on the goings on of a young country solicitor. A sort of legal James Herriot. Sadly it did not enjoy the same success though the photography was excellent. The opening credits were shown over the view just described. Ah yes, the title, "The Carnforth Practice".

Where the road swings right beneath dense foliage, look carefully for a permissive footpath on your left. There is a break in the wall with steps at the far side. A path leads down to the water's edge where a delightful shingle beach stretches away broken by trees including a couple of grand copper beech. Canada geese chewed nonchalantly at long grasses flanking the water.

Rydal from Loughrigg

At a kissing gate note the ha ha — sunken fence extending into the water. Beyond, woodland is entered, a high level path avoiding the shingle where the tide may well encroach in times of heavy rainfall. Woodland ends as abruptly as it began giving way to more shingle at the outfall of Grasmere at a weir maintaining a minimum level. A bridge spans the River Rothay providing a short cut back to the A591 for those with flagging limbs.

Take a track climbing easily above the main path, the latter's course parallel to the river. A wall swings in from the left to keep company. Soon the Loughrigg Terrace path is joined, this forming an alternative route leaving Red Bank at a higher point. A seat at the junction provides an excuse for a rest and to take in the view across to Nab Scar and down valley towards Ambleside. Refreshed, ignore a clear path descending, electing instead for one hugging the contour which passes yet another seat. The number of seats is in fact a feature of this walk, I must count them next time. Bracken is rampant in summer. Here I met the red shirts and having said good morning for the umpteenth time, paid attention discovering the occupants to be scouts from the U.S.A. on a U.K. tour.

Rough ground leads somewhat unexpectedly to the huge Loughrigg cave from which slate was quarried for many years. Wainwright remarks in his guide to the Central Fells that this will accommodate the entire population of Ambleside. During my many visits they have been noticeably absent, indeed on occasion I have had it to myself. Children will have a great time paddling through and falling into the shallow pools in its interior whilst parents stand and gawp.

Descend the swinging path from the caves mouth, re-entering woodland though first noting two further man-made caves at a lower level, these being less accessible. Rydal Water is glimpsed through trees, again with shingle beach, the lower path from the weir at Grasmere actually following the shoreline.

Our course takes a higher line via walled lane, which through a gate becomes metalled. Hidden in the woodlands on the right are two groups of cottages, hydrangea prominent in the gardens in season. Opposite the second group take to a signposted track left dropping steeply to a kissing gate. From here half right a narrow footbridge will be seen spanning the river. Cross it to exit on the busy A591. Glen Rothay Hotel is available for topping-up purposes in its beer garden — provided you can cross the road in one piece.

When replete follow the racetrack south for no more than 100 (thankful) yards to the sign for Rydal Mount via steep private road on your left, noting first in summer the magnificent standard fuschias in the garden of the cottage at the corner.

Ascend the hill past Rydal Church and the entrance to Dora's

Field. Higher yet is Rydal Hall where the diocese of Carlisle have a tea shop available to weary travellers. Rydal Mount, Wordsworth's main residence for the greater part of his life will repay a visit. During the winter months a combined excursion is offered organised by the Miss Cumbria Launch Co. based at Bowness. This takes in Brockhole the National Park Visitor Centre; Bowness and Rydal Mount under the banner, "Winter Wonderland". Wine at dusk in the old house by candlelight and log fire listening to a rendition of Wordsworth's poems appears to me a most civilised way to conclude a day.

Above Rydal Mount take to the bridleway on the left, bound for Grasmere. Hemmed in initially by walls, these soon give way to a clear track contouring the slopes of Nab Scar through bracken and mixed woodland, the rockface above being almost vertical in places. At one point a retaining wall has been erected to stabilize the fellside. A decaying forest is seen left, grotesque branchless sentinels waiting for a gale to topple them on to past fallen brethren. Two elderly walkers strode in the opposite direction, their rucksacks bleached by years of weather worn service. There are brambles a-plenty making this a good stretch during late summer and early autumn.

The bridleway widens at an isolated habitation, "Brockstone" to which there is vehicular access — just! At Dunnabeck, tarmac returns leading past a reedy pool flanked by rhododendrons and almost tropical vegetation.

A short step further and the lane descends towards Grasmere, a path right being signposted, "Alcock Tarn". For those still with energy to spare this walk may be extended to include that described in the next chapter, returning to Grasmere by an alternative route.

Should you have had enough for one day, continue on tarmac bearing right at a junction by another small pool to enter the village near Dove Cottage, crossing the A591 to return via B5287.

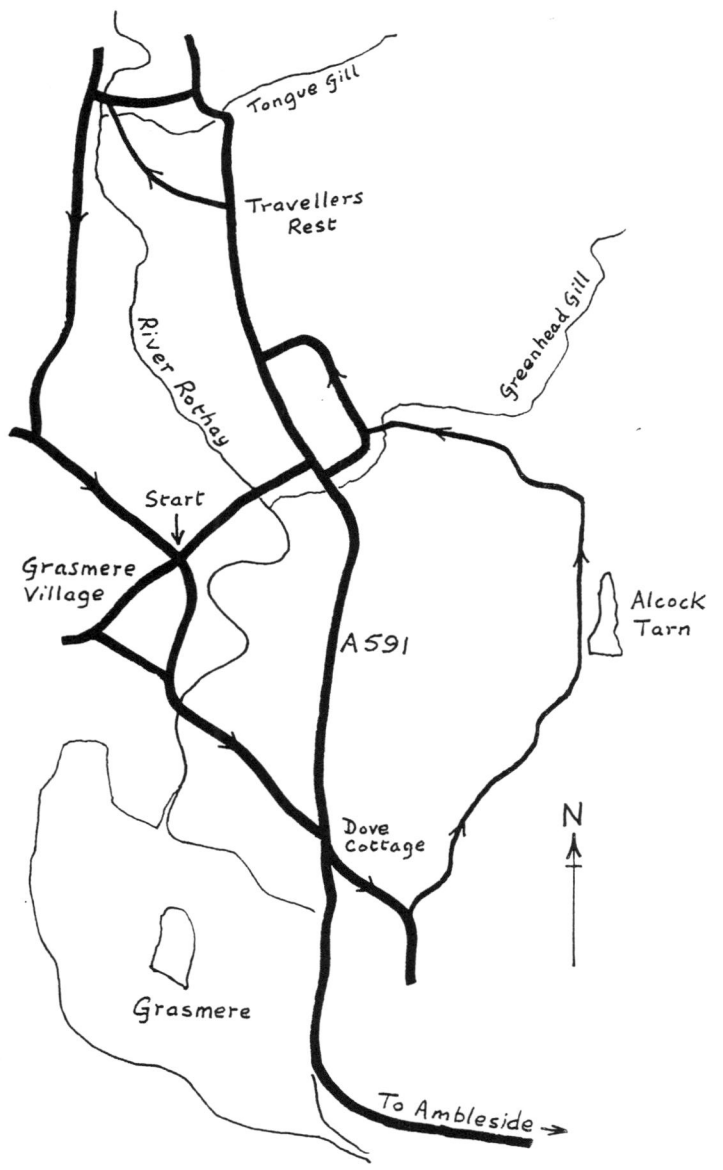

7. Alcock Tarn

Start and Finish: Grasmere village green. Leaving via Dove Cottage to climb to this man-made tarn on the 1200 foot contour. Returning by steep descent to Greenhead Gill and quiet lanes to the north of the village. This walk is an excellent introduction to the area with a bird's eye view into the Easedale and Greenburn valleys.
Distance: 4¼ miles.
Climbing: 1000 feet.
Time: 3 hours.
Map: O.S. English Lakes 1.25000 South East.
Public Transport: C.M.S. Routes 555; 556; 557. Lancaster/Keswick.

THE VILLAGE GREEN lies at the centre of Grasmere flanked by the Heaton Cooper studio and Sam Read's bookshop. There are seats a-plenty commemorating various events and past lovers of the area. From the door of the bookshop and facing the green, turn left to walk through the village, making a detour through the churchyard to view Wordsworth's grave in the far left corner. Cross the bridge by the tearoom where birds will happily join you at table almost taking food from your mouth. Continue to and cross the A591 to enter a quiet lane. Quiet, that is, apart from its first fifty yards or so on which tourists flock in their thousands to visit Dove Cottage, the best known Wordsworth shrine. At a reedy pool bear left still on tarmac to where a path is clearly signposted, "Alcock Tarn". There is a seat adjacent.

Ascend through bracken to a gateway where a National Trust sign proclaims this to be Brackenfell. At a bifurcation, climb steeply to the right accompanied by dry stone walls.

Above woodland, pause for breath at wrought iron gates set in the walls. Cameras out. Looking north east Helm Crag is flanked by the valleys of Easedale and Greenburn. A raven cronked by as I took in this scene on a recent visit. Across the wall is an alternative route to the tarn. Amazing how the grass the other side invariably appears greener. It isn't. Tackle another steep section until the gradient eases approaching the tarn.

Cross an unusual step stile built over a now immobile gate. From here first head for Grey Crag, a prominent viewpoint which on my last visit sported a red flag as did indeed several others in the vicinity. My initial reaction that the army had moved its ranges from Warcop proved unfounded. More likely they were markers for the famous Grasmere Fell Race.

Whatever, the view is worth the modest effort required to reach 1200 feet. From left to right take in Loughrigg Fell; Coniston Old

Man; Wetherlam; Great Carrs; Lingmoor; Pike O'Stickle; Silver Howe; Crinkle Crags; Bowfell; Harrison Stickle; Pavey Ark; High Raise; Ullscarf and Steel Fell. The latter was the scene of a minor fellwalking disaster for Stan and I on 15th February 1981 when, in gathering gloom, we found ourselves on the summit having taken a false bearing on the descent from Greenup Edge. As a result we gained not the Calf Crag/Gibson Knott ridge but that ascending Steel Fell. A fair step back to Grasmere by torchlight.

Since then we have continued our blunderings with slightly less error.

Alcock Tarn (spelt Allcock on the 2½ inch map) is man made, being dammed at its southern extremity to provide a greater reserve of water than originally retained by its shelf on the fellside. The water was used to power a mill at the Hollens, Grasmere. It is a popular spot for fishing and equally a butty. A mallard joined me in that function offering a vacuum-like facility in or out of the water in crumb clearing.

Leave at the north end of the tarn by a similar step stile to that at point of entry. The path descends Butter Crags by a series of zig zags improved in part by strategically placed steps of natural stone. Greenhead Gill swings in from the north to parallel our course albeit at lower elevation. Below, an aqueduct spans the beck carrying the Thirlmere pipeline to Manchester's thirsty water-users. Its course has now been healed by nature.

A seat, "In memory of Tennyson (Tim) Oldfield 1892–1978 author of, Come for a walk with me" provides respite for a view into the valley and Grasmere. A steep eroded section follows to the gill and footbridge at the head of a metalled lane serving Greenhead Tower and other properties. Continue on tarmac, the watercourse now much constricted will cause problems at times of heavy rain.

Meeting a loop from the A591, a left turn will lead easily via The Swan Hotel back to Grasmere. For a more interesting return take the opposite direction passing select properties to meet the main road which thankfully sports a footpath at this point. Head north towards The Travellers Rest. Should you be able to resist temptation, cross the road to a signposted path skirting a field. The path duly emerges at Low Mill Bridge though first stepping stones require careful negotiation over Tongue Gill prior to its confluence with Green Burn to form the River Rothay.

Follow the lane left, it being lined in summer with a goodly display of wild flowers, harebell; scabious; catmint and melancholy thistle to the fore. Later there will be an ample supply of blackberries.

Watch out for the milk tanker which treats the narrow lanes with a disdain born of long practice in confined spaces. There are many delightful cottages nestling amongst trees, before joining the lane from Easedale to cross Goody Bridge and emerge at the crossroads adjacent Grasmere village centre.

8. Great and Little Langdale

Start and Finish: Elterwater village. A circuit of Lingmoor Fell by field and fell through typical lakeland scenery surrounded by fine mountains. Uphill and downdale visiting both Great and Little Langdale. Some rough — not steep — sections plus a small amount of road walking on quiet lanes.
Distance: 8 miles.
Climbing: 800 feet.
Time: 5 hours but call it a full day.
Map: O.S. English Lakes 1.25000 South West.
Public Transport: C.M.S. Route 516 Ambleside–Dungeon Ghyll. (No Sunday service).

ELTERWATER village is approached via B5343 heading into Great Langdale from Skelwith Bridge. It has seen past industrial development and indeed there is still a huge quarry to the south of Great Langdale Beck. Free parking is available adjacent to the bowling green in the centre of this delightful village.

Cross the road bridge over Great Langdale Beck swinging left past Elterwater Country House Hotel. Bill, who suggested this particular walk, accompanied me whilst writing up the notes on what tuned out to be the one wet day during a protracted drought. He recalled some years back being in Great Langdale the morning following an exceptional gale. Many signposts had their arms blown round, a driver in his huge removal pantechnicon spending several hours trying to find his way to a job.

At a junction, go right passing Elterwater Hall on the left. When tarmacadam swings away right continue ahead on an ascending rough track unsuitable for cars or removal vans. Silver birch; holly and hawthorn line the way. A great spotted woodpecker called from amidst a stand of oaks. Willow warbler and jay were also in evidence whilst a robin sounded its alarm call.

At the brow there is a choice, elect for the cycle route descending open fellside to Dale End Farm where tarmac recommences. Parsley fern; raspberries; sloes; foxgloves and pink campion make a summer mixture in the hedgerow. The Little Langdale road may be seen below whilst opposite and prominent is Little Fell backed by Holme Fell. Cross the road, taking the track clearly marked for Birk House Farm. Little Langdale's reedy tarn is clearly seen during the descent to Slaters Bridge, there being a sign to the right of the farm.

The bridge itself is of the traditional pack horse type though handrails have been added. There are two flood arches to cope with the frequent torrents after heavy rain. It is therefore all the more surprising to find water lilies growing in this environment. Ascend to a walled lane, the topside of which is formed by spoil heaps from

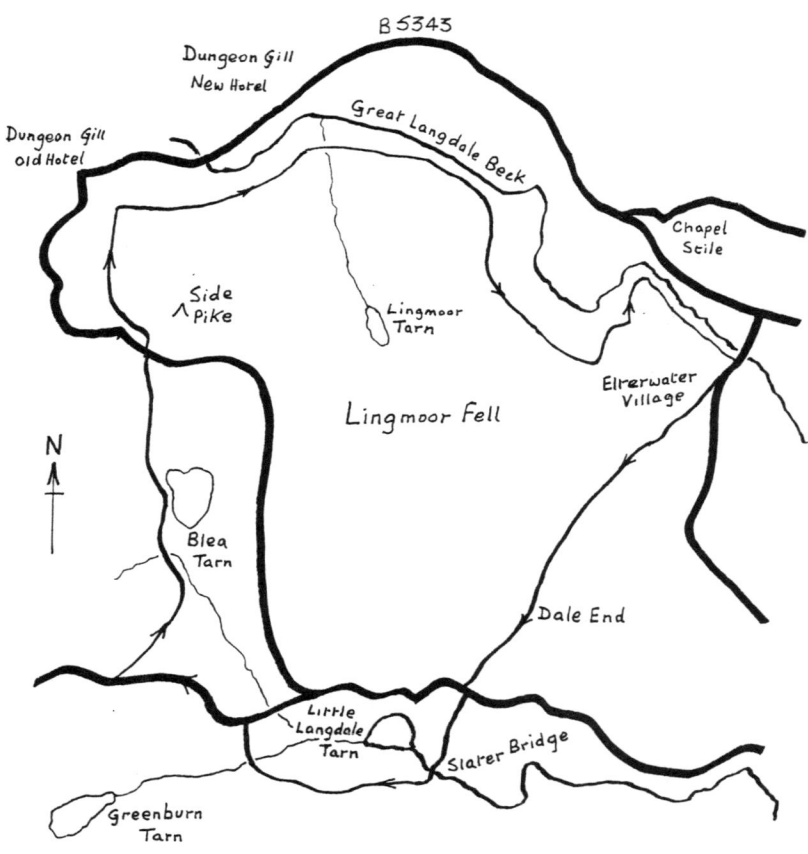

former slate quarries. This lane, down which it is just possible to manoeuvre a small vehicle — no removal vans, please — allows a sinuous access via Tilberthwaite Gill. Many years ago I tackled it from High Yewdale near Coniston in a Hillman Minx being under the mistaken impression that it led into Little Langdale. It does, by a ford across the River Brathay which at the time was a raging torrent. I recall debouching the family with instructions that when I tackled the rough ravine down which the car had just bounced, they should push like hell and I would wait for them at he top. Needless to say we escaped, which simply goes to show how versatile a company car can be!

Hall Garth, a National Trust property, has a glorious rock garden and around the corner on a barn roof a huge clump of sempervivum. Cars parked close by appear to indicate the rough approach has possibly been eased. High Hall Garth most definitely has no vehicular access and beyond the open fell is regained. Bog asphodel and bell heather were in evidence as we passed, the former almost a summer daffodil.

Confusion may occur where the path forks, the sign indicating footpath left. This is however the route for Greenburn and Wetside Edge. Go right, Pike O'Blisco being the dominant height ahead. Cross Greenburn Beck at Bridge End to regain the road at Fell Foot. Turning left, in due course pass the farm of same name which literally encroaches on the highway, a bedroom overhanging it. Another place for removal vans to avoid.

Follow the road, now ascending, a low grassy mound to its left. This is a THING mound, a former outdoor assembly point for Norse folk. Continue upward, skirting Castle Howe on your right until the view is clear across to the Langdale Pikes, possibly at their best on an autumn day with a sea of bracken aglow beneath a low sun. A track will be seen to leave the road further ahead, contour the lower slopes of Pike O'Blisco and head for Blea Tarn. Resist the temptation to take a bee line as presumably you neither fly nor possess webbed feet. Incidentally, the road continuing over the Wrynose and Hardknott passes is the steepest in the country. On a January day some fifteen years ago I attempted to reach Wrynose summit from which to start a walk, once again in a company car. Company cars, you should understand, travel faster — both forward and reverse — than conventional models and tackle terrain at which a tractor would blanch. At Wrynose Bridge I struck black ice, the car sliding sideways. It was nearly a case of abandon ship. After a thirteen point turn, car and I thankfully slithered into a downward facing posture just as the mountain rescue landrover spitting and snarling roared past negotiating the ice before disappearing summitward.

Through Blea Moss the rough track contours the foot of Pike O'Blisco to cross the head of a ravine into which tumbles Bleamoss Beck to the right of an enormous boulder. Bell heather grows from crevices inaccessible to the Herdwicks.

A gate gives access to woodland adjoining Blea Tarn. Ignore a wooden bridge, instead bearing left. Although this is very much a mixed wood the prevailing species is rhododendron forming a tunnel through which the path meanders. The effect is amazonian yet rhododendrons are natives of Asia being in abundance in the Himalayas. Should hunger call, the tarn shore forms an ideal butty stop beneath the mantle framing Lingmoor. Kids can meantime explore the enchanted wood.

The wood terminates just as abruptly at another gate. From here, Pike O'Stickle and Gimmer Crag dominate the horizon whilst closer to hand Side Pike forms the terminus to Lingmoor.

Bog asphodel is again profuse on a juicy crossing to meet the road linking the two Langdales at a cattle grid. Opposite, climb a step stile to find some twenty yards beyond a slate seat bearing the inscription "William Herbert Brown, Burton-on-Trent 1880–1938". Just before my time. Descend a steep path, initially parallel to the road, the entire Langdale range now in view. Way below, the Old Dungeon Ghyll Hotel gives scale to the scene. Bill and I noted the tapestry of newly mown hay meadows.

Doubt may occur near Side House. After climbing a stile and crossing a recent plank bridge, the track descends, another bridge invitingly placed on the left. Ignore this, continuing instead ahead to climb where a sign indicates a new track. The site of a former croft is found, with higher yet a tree-clothed ravine which, if followed, would lead to Lingmoor Tarn. There are however easier ways to the tarn which on a good day is well worth a visit.

We noticed now a knot of folk descending the opposite fellside carrying a stretcher. Presumably a climbing accident. Bill, an early member of the cave rescue organisation at Clapham in the Yorkshire Dales recounted how on one of the early rescues, a door was commandeered for the occasion, doubling as a stretcher before later being returned to its hinges. Volunteer rescuers were generally co-opted as required from the Masons Arms in those early days.

Below, Langdale Beck is canalised, a preventative measure against flooding. Approaching Oak Howe by walled lane, take care at the old barn to bear right, an alternative route also being signposted here. Within 100 yards a further sign will give reassurance. Very soon woodland is again encountered and a metalled lane.

At Baysbrown Farm sheep had recently been smitten, unfortunately, the persistent drizzle having meantime changed for the worse, sheep and lambs alike wore orange coats where the dye had run over freshly shorn bodies.

You may with ease continue along the lane to where it meets the outward route. However, should you wish to see a little of Lakeland's heavy industry, bear left down a signposted bridleway passing through the Elterwater Slate quarry workings. Huge tractors, wheels permanently chained stood idle on our last visit during the period of annual closure. the slate is widely in demand, we have an Elterwater green fireplace in our home.

The main quarry road accompanies Great Langdale Beck to the village, on the opposite bank a timeshare development being sheltered by woodland. So ends a fascinating day's trek through the very heart of central lakeland, in the process circumventing Lingmoor Fell.

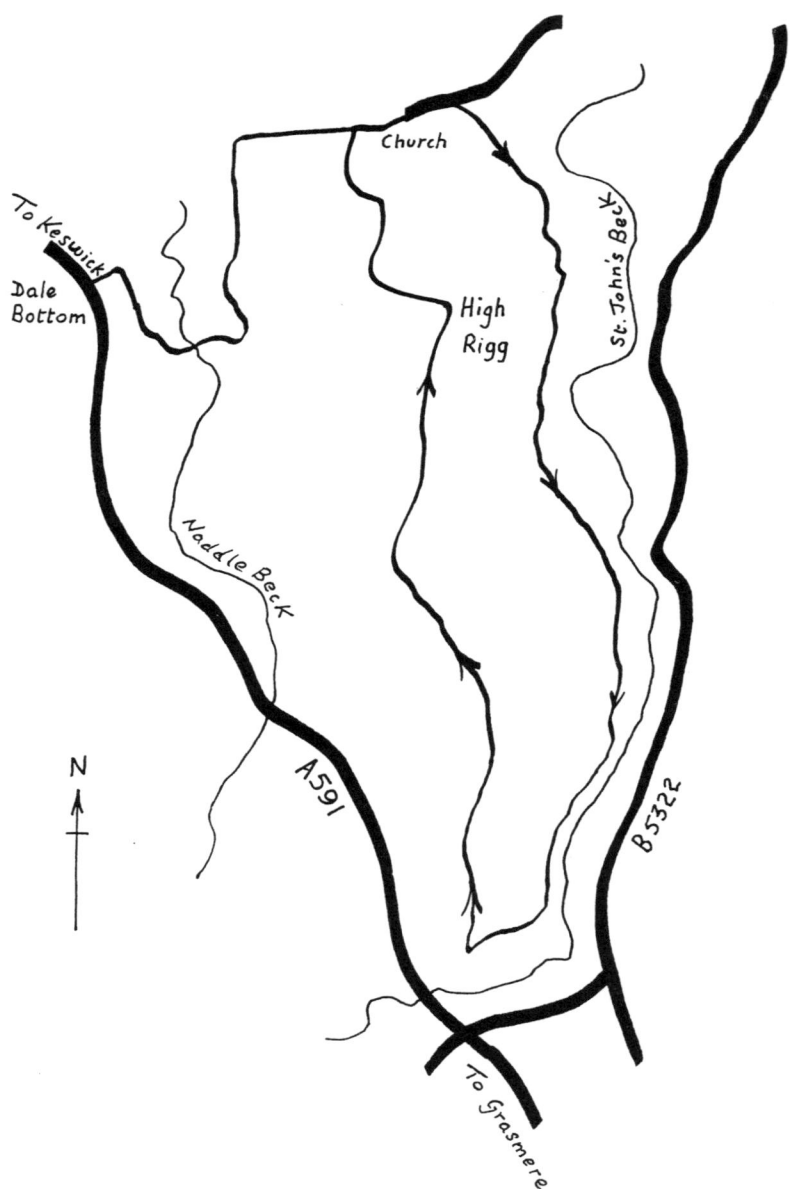

9. The Vale of St John's and High Rigg

Start and Finish: St John's in the Vale church midway between Dale Bottom 3 miles South East of Keswick and Wanthwaite 2½ miles South of Threlkeld.
Distance: 5½ miles.
Climbing: 1000 feet.
Time: 3½ hours.
Map: O.S. English Lakes 1.25000 North West.
Public Transport: C.M.S. Routes 555; 556; 557 – Alight Dale Bottom. Note this adds a further 2½ miles to the expedition. If travelling by private transport the only tarmac approach is from the east and single track for the last ¾ mile.

THIS walk is really an extension of number one, tackling on the return leg the exhilarating traverse of High Rigg. Accomplished this way, Blencathra will be viewed to best advantage on a clear day.

With a bungaloid structure on your left and the church with its extended graveyard on your right enter a descending path at a sign, "Bridleway St John in the Vale". Opposite is the great mass of Clough head, the northern terminus of the Dodds. The descent is easy, accompanied by a wall on your left overhung by oaks. St John's Beck is in view with the B5322 beyond. Thankfully this road is still relatively quiet. Scree tumbles from High Rigg, the scene being dramatic. Levels of the former Bramcrag Quarry can be seen and the course of the mineral railway which connected with standard gauge interchange facilities on the C.K.P.R. (Cockermouth, Keswick and Penrith Railway) east of Threlkeld station some 2¼™ miles distant. The Threlkeld Granite Co. Ltd. was a major employer of labour until 1940. Thereafter followed a steady decline until final closure in 1982.

The scenery has a distinctly Scottish flavour as our route skirts the flank of the fell, uphill and downdale. As Bill pointed out, this is somewhat frustrating when you are used to gaining height early morning, not descending overmuch until returning late afternoon.

The vale becomes more constricted as stunted hawthorn litter the path. Higher, bracken and herdwicks abound. Foxgloves sprouted in the early spring sunshine whilst a chaffinch called cheerily. Castle Rock of Triermain comes into view beyond a packhorse bridge spanning the now canalised beck. The density of woodland increases, orange tints of larch forming a haze in the middle distance. A recent conifer plantation is to hand, Norway Spruce, our popular Christmas Tree. A pocket tree guide will be of assistance on this outward leg. Catkins were in evidence and Bill also pointed out mini species of Lodge Pole Pine which apparently red Indians use as tent poles. This area is not unlike Loughrigg Terrace.

Past Low Bridgend the path runs in parallel to the beck across which an extensive timberyard will be seen. Abruptly the path climbs steeply to take a course through larch defying gravity in their precarious siting. Swinging west the roar of the beck gives way to that of traffic as the A591 bursts upon the scene, bisected here by a minor road heading for Thirlmere dam.

Note carefully a track inclining right seeking the ridge. This is a gem. Stop frequently to appreciate the expanding view, kidding yourself it is not really a case of lack of breath. Notice that the road bridge spanning the beck is of red sandstone, more reminiscent of the Kirkoswald area of East Cumbria. Topped by pines and overlooking Thirlmere stands the precipice of Raven Crag, another grand viewpoint. Stan and I spent a half day trying to find a way beyond and across Shouthwaite Gill. There isn't one. So be told.

The track climbs steadily amongst a sea of bracken heading towards pines crowning the ridge. Retrospectively Thirlmere is flanked on the left by the Dodds, still capped in snow on this visit. Castle Crag of Triermain as immortalised by Sir Walter Scott in "The Bride of Triermain" no longer presents its pose of impregnability as seen from the valley.

Reaching the southern end of the ridge Blencathra may be revealed in all its majesty. The track undulates, passing a small tarn which will possibly dry up during a period of drought. A larger tarn in a pocket of the fell will be found in the lea of a drystone wall. Now the notoriously wet central ridge running from Bleaberry Fell to Ullscarf is clearly seen.

Aim north west for a stile left of a T-junction of walls. From here a clear track parallels the north running wall until this abruptly descends eastward. Continue ahead.

At the next col take in the view north west over Bassenthwaite Lake — the only one in the district — Grisedale Pike and the Wythop Fells to its left with Dodd Wood leading to the Skiddaw massif right and Latrigg crouching in the near foreground. The summit of High Rigg is unmistakable, a rocky knoll amidst the sea of grass. It is a popular picnic spot, the more so with the hordes of young folk ascending from the Diocesan Youth Centre adjacent the church.

An easy swinging descent is made over velvet turf, Tewet Tarn in the middle distance mirroring Blencathra on a still day. Notice that St John's church tower is simply yet effectively castellated by a selection of suitably shaped stones placed on its near flat top.

Pass through a stile to gain the road via the rear of the youth centre to conclude a satisfying exploration of St John's Vale and High Rigg.